FOR TO END YET AGAIN

From the same publishers

Samuel Beckett

Novels

Dream of Fair to Middling Women (1932)
Murphy (1938)
Watt (1945)
First Love (1945)
Mercier and Camier (1946)
Molloy (1951)*
Malone Dies (1951)*

The Unnamable (1953) *
How It Is (1961)
Company (1980)**
Ill Seen Ill Said (1981)**
Worstward Ho (1983)**

* published together as the Trilogy
** published together as Nohow On

Short Prose

More Pricks than Kicks (1934)
Collected Short Prose (in preparation)
Beckett Shorts (see below)

Poetry

Collected Poems (1930-1978)
Anthology of Mexican Poetry
        (translations)

Criticism

Proust & Three Dialogues with Georges Duthuit (1931,1949)
Disjecta (1929-1967)

Beckett Shorts (A collection of 12 short volumes to commemorate the writer's death in 1989)

1. Texts for Nothing (1947-52)
2. Dramatic Works and Dialogues (1938-67)
3. All Strange Away (1963)
4. Worstward Ho (1983)
5. Six Residua (1957-72)
6. For to End Yet Again (1960-75)

7. The Old Tune (1962)
8. First Love (1945)
9. As the Story Was Told
10. Three Novellas (1945-6)
11. Stirrings Still (1986-9)
12. Selected Poems (1930-85)

FOR TO END YET AGAIN

Samuel Beckett

John Calder
London

This edition first published 1999 in Great Britain by
John Calder Publishers
London
First general edition published in Great Britain by
John Calder Publishers (London), 1975
Originally published in French, individually in *Minuit* and together as *Pour Finir Encore et autres foirades* by Editions de Minuit, Paris, 1976.
Still first published by Calder & Boyars London, 1975
Five Fizzles first published in English by Petersburg Press, London 1976.
For to End Yet Again first published in *New Writing and Writers 13*, 1976 by John Calder Publishers.

© all material in this volume Samuel Beckett Estate, 1999
© Les Editions de Minuit, 1970

ISBN 0 7145 36008
Paperback

British Library Cataloguing in Publication Data
A catalogue record for this title is available from the British Library

Printed in Canada by Webcom Ltd

CONTENTS

5

INTRODUCTION

For To End Yet Again was written in 1975 and first published as *Pour finir encore* by Editions de Minuit in 1976.

Still was written in English 1973, and first published in 1974 with etchings by William Hayter (M'Arte Edizione, Milan, editor Luigi M Majno) and 1975 in John Calder's Signature Anthology (Calder and Boyars) 1975.

Other Fizzles written circa 1960 and translated 1973–4, appearing in the review *Minuit* and later in *Pour finir encore* (Editions de Minuit).

Afar A Bird first appeared in 1973 with etchings by Avigdor Arikha (Double Elephant Press, New York) under the title *Au loin un oiseau*.

Closed Space is a condensed version (1975) of a much longer work in French begun 1968 and finally abandoned. Translated 1975 by the author from *Se voir* (with *Pour finir encore*, Editions de Minuit 1976).

Five Fizzles first appeared in English with etchings by Jasper Johns (Petersburg Press, London, editor Peter Cornwall Jones) in 1976 in advance of the present publication.

The French title for the same collection is *Pour finir encore* et autres foirades (Ed. du Minuit 1976).

7

FOR TO END
YET AGAIN

FOR to end yet again skull alone in a dark place pent bowed on a board to begin. Long thus to begin till the place fades followed by the board long after. For to end yet again skull alone in the dark the void no neck no face just the box last place of all in the dark the void. Place of remains where once used to gleam in the dark on and off used to glimmer a remain. Remains of the days of the light of day never light so faint as theirs so pale. Thus then the skull makes to glimmer again in lieu of going out. There in the end all at once or by degrees there dawns and magic lingers a leaden dawn. By degrees less dark till final grey or all at once as if switched on grey sand as far as eye can see beneath grey cloudless sky same grey. Skull last place of all black void within without till all at once or by degrees this leaden dawn at last checked no sooner dawned. Grey cloudless sky grey sand as far as eye can see long desert to begin. Sand pale as dust ah but dust indeed deep to engulf the haughtiest monuments which too it once was here and there. There in the end same grey invisible to any other eye stark erect amidst his ruins the expelled. Same grey all that little body from head to feet sunk ankle deep were it not for the eyes last bright of all. The arms still cleave to the trunk and to each other the legs made for flight. Grey cloudless sky ocean of dust not a ripple mock confines verge upon verge hell air not a breath. Mingling with the dust slowly sinking some almost fully sunk the ruins of the refuge. First change of all in the end a fragment comes away and falls. With slow fall for so dense a body it lights like cork on water and scarce breaks the surface. Thus then the skull last place of all makes to glimmer again in lieu of going out. Grey cloudless sky verge upon verge grey timeless air of those nor for God nor for his enemies. There again in the end way amidst the verges a light in the grey two white dwarfs. Long at first mere whiteness from afar they toil step by step through the grey dust linked by a litter same white seen from above in the grey air. Slowly it sweeps the dust so bowed the backs and long the arms compared with the legs and deep sunk the feet. Bleached as one same wilderness they are so alike the eye cannot tell them apart. They carry face to face and relay each other often so that turn about they backward lead the way. His who follows who knows to shape the course much as the coxwain with light touch the skiff. Let him veer to the north or other cardinal point and promptly the other by as much to the antipode. Let one stop short and the other about this pivot slew the litter through a semi-circle and thereon the roles are reversed. Bone white of the sheet seen from above and the shafts fore and aft and the dwarfs to the crowns of their massy skulls. From time to time impelled as one they let fall the litter then again as one take it up again without having to stoop. It is the dung litter of laughable memory with shafts twice as long as the couch. Swelling the sheet now fore now aft as permutations list a pillow marks the place of the head. At the end of the arms the four hands open as one and the litter so close to the dust already settles without a sound. Monstrous extremities including skulls stunted legs and trunks monstrous arms stunted faces. In the end the feet as one lift clear the left forward backward the right and the amble resumes. Grey dust as far as eye can see beneath grey cloudless sky and there all at once or by degrees this whiteness to decipher. Yet to imagine if he can see it the last expelled amidst his ruins if he can ever see it and seeing believe his eyes. Between him and it bird's-eye view the space grows no less but has only even now appeared last desert to be crossed. Little body last stage of all stark erect still amidst his ruins all silent and marble still. First change of all a fragment comes away from mother ruin and with slow fall scarce stirs the dust. Dust having engulfed so much it can engulf no more and woe the little on the surface still. Or mere digestive torpor as once the boas which past with one last gulp clean sweep at last. Dwarfs distant whiteness sprung from nowhere motionless afar in the grey air where dust alone possible. Wilderness and carriage immemorial as one they advance as one retreat hither thither halt move on again. He facing forward will sometimes halt and hoist as best he can his head as if to scan the void and who knows alter course. Then on so soft the eye does not see them go driftless with heads sunk and lidded eyes. Long lifted to the horizontal faces closer and closer strain as it will the eye achieves no more than two tiny oval blanks. Atop the cyclopean dome rising sheer from jut of brow yearns white to the grey sky the bump of habitativity or love of home. Last change of all in the end the expelled falls headlong down and lies back to sky full little stretch amidst his ruins. Feet centre body radius falls unbending as a statue falls faster and faster the space of a quadrant. Eagle the eye that shall discern him now mingled with the ruins mingling with the dust beneath a sky forsaken of its scavengers. Breath has not left him though soundless still and exhaling scarce ruffles the dust. Eyes in their orbits blue still unlike the doll's the fall has not shut nor yet the dust stopped up. No fear henceforth of his ever having not to believe them before that whiteness afar where sky and dust merge. Whiteness neither on earth nor above of the dwarfs as if at the end of their trials the litter left lying between them the white bodies marble still. Ruins all silent marble still little body prostrate at attention wash blue deep in gaping sockets. As in the days erect the arms still cleave to the trunk and to each other the legs made for flight. Fallen unbending all his little length as though pushed from behind by some helping hand or by the wind but not a breath. Or murmur from some dreg of life after the lifelong stand fall fall never fear no fear of your rising again. Sepulchral skull is this then its last state all set for always litter and dwarfs ruins

14

and little body grey cloudless sky glutted dust verge upon verge hell air not a breath. And dream of a way in a space with neither here nor there where all the footsteps ever fell can never fare nearer to anywhere nor from anywhere further away. No for in the end for to end yet again by degrees or as though switched on dark falls there again that certain dark that alone certain ashes can. Through it who knows yet another end beneath a cloudless sky same dark it earth and sky of a last end if ever there had to be another absolutely had to be.

STILL

BRIGHT at last close of a dark day the sun shines out at last and goes down. Sitting quite still at valley window normally turn head now and see it the sun low in the southwest sinking. Even get up certain moods and go stand by western window quite still watching it sink and then the afterglow. Always quite still some reason some time past this hour at open window facing south in small upright wicker chair with armrests. Eyes stare out unseeing till first movement some time past close though unseeing still while still light. Quite still again then all quite quiet apparently till eyes open again while still light though less. Normally turn head now ninety degrees to watch sun which if already gone then fading afterglow. Even get up certain moods and go stand by western window till quite dark and even some evenings some reason long after. Eyes then open again while still light and close again in what if not quite a single movement almost. Quite still again then at open window facing south over the valley in this wicker chair though actually close inspection not still at all but trembling all over. Close inspection namely detail by detail all over to add up finally to this whole not still at all but trembling all over. But casually in this failing light impression dead still even the hands clearly trembling and the breast faint rise and fall. Legs side by side broken right angles at the knees as in that old statue some old god twanged at sunrise and again at sunset. Trunk likewise dead plumb right up to top of skull seen from behind including nape clear of chairback. Arms likewise broken right angles at the elbows forearms along armrests just right length forearms and rests for hands clenched lightly to rest on ends. So quite still again then all quite quiet apparently eyes closed which to anticipate when they open again if they do in time then dark or some degree of starlight or moonlight or both. Normally watch night fall however long from this narrow chair or standing by western window quite still either case. Quite still namely staring at some one thing alone such as tree or bush a detail alone if near if far the whole if far enough till it goes. Or by eastern window certain moods staring at some point on the hillside such as that beech in whose shade once quite still till it goes. Chair some reason always same place same position facing south as though clamped down whereas in reality no lighter no more movable imaginable. Or anywhere any ope staring out at nothing just failing light quite still till quite dark though of course no such thing just less light still when less did not seem possible. Quite still then all this time eyes open when discovered then closed then opened and closed again no other movement any kind though of course not still at all when suddenly or so it looks this movement impossible to follow let alone describe. The right hand slowly opening leaves the armrest taking with it the whole forearm complete with elbow and slowly rises opening further as it goes and turning a little deasil till midway to the head it hesitates and hangs half open trembling in mid air. Hangs there as if half inclined to return that is sink back slowly closing as it goes and turning the other way till as and where it began clenched lightly on end of rest. Here because of what comes now not midway to the head but almost there before it hesitates and hangs there trembling as if half inclined etc. Half no but on the verge when in its turn the head moves from its place forward and down among the ready fingers where no sooner received and held it weighs on down till elbow meeting armrest brings this last movement to an end and all still once more. Here back a little way to that suspense before head to rescue as if hand's need the greater and on down in what if not quite a single movement almost till elbow against rest. All quite still again then head in hand namely thumb on outer edge of right socket index ditto left and middle on left cheekbone plus as the hours pass lesser contacts each more or less now more now less with the faint stirrings of the various parts as night wears on. As if even in the dark eyes closed not enough and perhaps even more than ever necessary against that no such thing the further shelter of the hand. Leave it so all quite still or try listening to the sounds all quite still head in hand listening for a sound.

21

HE IS BAREHEAD

HE is barehead, barefoot, clothed in a singlet and tight trousers too short for him, his hands have told him so, again and again, and his feet, feeling each other and rubbing against the legs, up and down calves and shins. To this vaguely prison garb none of his memories answer, so far, but all are of heaviness, in this connexion, of fullness and of thickness. The great head where he toils is all mockery, he is forth again, he'll be back again. Some day he'll see himself, his whole front, from the chest down, and the arms, and finally the hands, first rigid at arm's length, then close up, trembling, to his eyes. He halts, for the first time since he knows he's under way, one foot before the other, the higher flat, the lower on its toes, and waits for a decision. Then he moves on. Spite of the dark he does not grope his way, arms outstretched, hands agape and the feet held back just before the ground. With the result he must often, namely at every turn, strike against the walls that hem his path, against the right-hand when he turns left, the left-hand when he turns right, now with his foot, now with the crown of his head, for he holds himself bowed, because of the rise, and because he always holds himself bowed, his back humped, his head thrust forward, his eyes cast down. He loses his blood, but in no great quantity, the little wounds have time to close before being opened again, his pace is so slow. There are places where the walls almost meet, then it is the shoulders take the shock. But instead of stopping short, and even turning back, saying to himself, This is the end of the road, nothing now but to return to the other terminus and start again, instead he attacks the narrow sideways and so finally squeezes through, to the great hurt of his chest and back. Do his eyes, after such long exposure to the gloom, begin to pierce it? No, and this is one of the reasons why he shuts them more and more, more and more often and for ever longer spells. For his concern is increasingly to spare himself needless fatigue, such as that come of staring before him, and even all about him, hour after hour, day after day, and never seeing a thing. This is not the time to go into his wrongs, but perhaps he was wrong not to persist, in his efforts to pierce the gloom. For he might well have succeeded, in the end, up to a point, which would have brightened things up for him, nothing like a ray of light, from time to time, to brighten things up for one. And all may yet grow light, at any moment, first dimly and then – how can one say? – then more and more, till all is flooded with light, the way, the ground, the walls, the vault, without his being one whit the wiser. The moon may appear, framed at the end of the vista, and he in no state to rejoice and quicken his step, or on the contrary wheel and run, while there is yet time. For the moment however no complaints, which is the main. The legs notably seem in good shape, that is a blessing, Murphy had first-rate legs. The head is still a little weak, it needs time to get going again, that part does. No sign of insanity in any case, that is a blessing. Meagre equipment, but well balanced. The heart? No complaints. It's going again, enough to see him through. But see how now, having turned right for example, instead of turning left a little further on he turns right again. And see how now again, yet a little further on, instead of turning left at last he turns right yet again. And so on until, instead of turning right yet again, as he expected, he turns left at last. Then for a time his zigzags resume their tenor, deflecting him alternately to right and left, that is to say bearing him onward in a straight line more or less, but no longer the same straight line as when he set forth, or rather as when he suddenly realized he was forth, or perhaps after all the same. For if there are long periods when the right predominates, there are others when the left prevails. It matters little in any case, so long as he keeps on climbing. But see how now a little further on the ground falls away so sheer that he has to rear violently backward in order not to fall. Where is it then that life awaits him, in relation to his starting-point, to the point rather at which he suddenly realized he was started, above or below? Or will they cancel out in the end, the long gentle climbs and headlong steeps? It matters little in any case, so long as he is on the right road, and that

27

he is, for there are no others, unless he has let them slip by unnoticed, one after another. Walls and ground, if not of stone, are no less hard, to the touch, and wet. The former, certain days, he stops to lick. The fauna, if any, is silent. The only sounds, apart from those of the body on its way, are of fall, a great drop dropping at last from a great height and bursting, a solid mass that leaves its place and crashes down, lighter particles collapsing slowly. Then the echo is heard, as loud at first as the sound that woke it and repeated sometimes a good score of times, each time a little weaker, no, sometimes louder than the time before, till finally it dies away. Then silence again, broken only by the sound, intricate and faint, of the body on its way. But such sounds of fall are not common and mostly silence reigns, broken only by the sounds of the body on its way, of the bare feet on the wet ground, of the laboured breathing, of the body striking against the walls or squeezing through the narrows, of the clothes, singlet and trousers, espousing and resisting the movements of the body, coming unstuck from the damp flesh and sticking to it again, tattering and fluttered where in tatters already by sudden flurries as suddenly stilled, and finally of the hands as now and then they pass, back and forth, over all those parts of the body they can reach without fatigue. He himself has yet to drop. The air is foul. Sometimes he halts and leans against a wall, his feet wedged against the other. He has already a number of memories, from the memory of the day he suddenly knew he was there, on this same path still bearing him along, to that now of having halted to lean against the wall, he has a little past already, even a smatter of settled ways. But it is all still fragile. And often he surprises himself, both moving and at rest, but more often moving, for he seldom comes to rest, as destitute of history as on that first day, on this same path, which is his beginning, on days of great recall. But usually now, the surprise once past, memory returns and takes him back, if he will, far back to that first instant beyond which nothing, when he was already old, that is to say near to death, and knew, though unable to recall having lived, what age and death are, with other momentous matters. But it is all still fragile. And often he suddenly begins, in these black windings, and makes his first steps for quite a while before realizing they are merely the last, or latest. The air is so foul that only he seems fitted to survive it who never breathed the other, the true life-giving, or so long ago as to amount to never. And such true air, coming hard on that of here, would very likely prove fatal, after a few lungfuls. But the change from one to the other will no doubt be gentle, when the time comes, and gradual, as the man draws closer and closer to the open. And perhaps even now the air is less foul than when he started, then when he suddenly realized he was started. In any case little by little his history takes shape, with if not yet exactly its good days and bad, at least studded with occasions passing rightly or wrongly for outstanding, such as the straitest narrow, the loudest fall, the most lingering collapse, the steepest descent, the greatest number of successive turns the same way, the greatest fatigue, the longest rest, the longest – aside from the sound of the body on its way – silence. Ah yes, and the most rewarding passage of the hands, on the one hand, the feet, on the other, over all those parts of the body within their reach. And the sweetest wall lick. In a word all the summits. Then other summits, hardly less elevated, such as a shock so rude that it rivalled the rudest of all. Then others still, scarcely less eminent, a wall lick so sweet as to vie with the second sweetest. Then little or nothing of note till the minima, these two unforgettable, on days of great recall, a sound of fall so muted by the distance, or for want of weight, or for lack of space between departure and arrival, that it was perhaps his fancy. Or again, second example, no, not a good example. Other landmarks still are provided by first times, and even second. Thus the first narrow, for example, no doubt because he was not expecting it, impressed him quite as strongly as the straitest, just as the second collapse, no doubt because he was expecting it, was no less than the briefest never to be forgotten. So with one thing and another little by little his history takes shape, and even changes shape, as new maxima and minima tend to cast into the shade, and toward oblivion, those momentarily glorified, and as fresh elements and motifs, such as these bones of which more very shortly, and at length, in view of their importance, contribute to enrich it.

HORN CAME ALWAYS

HORN came always at night. I received him in the dark. I had come to bear everything bar being seen. In the beginning I would send him away after five or six minutes. Till he learnt to go of his own accord, once his time was up. He consulted his notes by the light of an electric torch. Then he switched it off and spoke in the dark. Light silence, dark speech. It was five or six years since anyone had seen me, to begin with myself. I mean the face I had pored over so, all down the years. Now I would resume that inspection, that it may be a lesson to me, in my mirrors and looking-glasses so long put away. I'll let myself be seen before I'm done. I'll call out, if there is a knock, Come in! But I speak now of five or six years ago. These allusions to now, to before and after, and all such yet to come, that we may feel ourselves in time. I had more trouble with the body proper. I masked it as best I could, but when I got out of bed it was sure to show. For I was now beginning, then if you prefer, to get out of bed again. Then there is the matter of its injuries. But the body was of less consequence.

Whereas the face, no, not at any price. Hence Horn at night. When he forgot his torch he made shift with matches. Were I to ask, for example, And her gown that day?, then he switched on, thumbed through his notes, found the particular, switched off and answered, for example, The yellow. He did not like one to interrupt him and I must confess I seldom had call to. Interrupting him one night I asked him to light his face. He did so, briefly, switched off and resumed the thread. Interrupting again I asked him to be silent for a moment. That night things went no further. But the next, or more likely the next but one, I desired him at the outset to light his face and keep it lit till further notice. The light, bright at first, gradually died down to no more than a yellow glimmer which then, to my surprise, persisted undiminished some little while. Then suddenly it was dark again and Horn went away, the five or six minutes having presumably expired. But here one of two things, either the final extinction had coincided, by some prank of chance, with the close of the session, or else Horn, knowing his time to be up, had cut off the last dribs of current. I still see, sometimes, that waning face disclosing, more and more clearly the more it entered shadow, the one I remembered. In the end I said to myself, as unaccountably it lingered on, No doubt about it, it is he. It is in outer space, not to be confused with the other, that such images develop. I need only interpose my hand, or close my eyes, to banish them, or take off my eyeglasses for them to fade. This is a help, but not a real protection, as we shall see. I try to keep before me therefore, as far as possible, when I get up, some such unbroken plane as that which I command from my bed, I mean the ceiling. For I have taken to getting up again. I thought I had made my last journey, the one I must now try once more to elucidate, that it may be a lesson to me, the one from which it were better I had never returned. But the feeling gains on me that I must undertake another. So I have taken to getting up again and making a few steps in the room, holding on to the bars of the bed. What ruined me at bottom was athletics. With all that jumping and running when I was young, and even long after in the case of certain events, I wore out the machine before its time. My fortieth year had come and gone and I still throwing the javelin.

AFAR A BIRD

AFAR A BIRD

RUINSTREWN land, he has trodden it all night long, I gave up, hugging the hedges, between road and ditch, on the scant grass, little slow steps, no sound, stopping ever and again, every ten steps say, little wary steps, to catch his breath, then listen, ruin-strewn land, I gave up before birth, it is not possible otherwise, but birth there had to be, it was he, I was inside, now he stops again, for the hundredth time that night say, that gives the distance gone, it's the last, hunched over his stick, I'm inside, it was he who wailed, he who saw the light, I didn't wail, I didn't see the light, one on top of the other the hands weigh on the stick, the head weighs on the hands, he has caught his breath, he can listen now, the trunk horizontal, the legs asprawl, sagging at the knees, same old coat, the stiffened tails stick up behind, day dawns, he has only to raise his eyes, open his eyes, raise his eyes, he merges in the hedge, afar a bird, a moment past he grasps and is fled, it was he had a life, I didn't have a life, a life not worth having, because of me, it's impossible I should have a mind and I have one, someone divines me, divines us,

that's what he's come to, come to in the end, I see
him in my mind, there divining us, hands and head
a little heap, the hours pass, he is still, he seeks a
voice for me, it's impossible I should have a voice
and I have none, he'll find one for me, ill beseeming
me, it will meet the need, his need, but no more of
him, that image, the little heap of hands and head,
the trunk horizontal, the jutting elbows, the eyes
closed and the face rigid listening, the eyes hidden
and the whole face hidden, that image and no more,
never changing, ruinstrewn land, night recedes, he
is fled, I'm inside, he'll do himself to death, because
of me, I'll live it with him, I'll live his death, the end
of his life and then his death, step by step, in the
present, how he'll go about it, it's impossible I
should know, I'll know, step by step, it's he will die,
I won't die, there will be nothing of him left but
bones, I'll be inside, nothing but a little grit, I'll be
inside, it is not possible otherwise, ruinstrewn land,
he is fled through the hedge, no more stopping now,
he will never say I, because of me, he won't speak to
anyone, no one will speak to him, he won't speak to
himself, there is nothing left in his head, I'll feed it
all it needs, all it needs to end, to say I no more, to
open its mouth no more, confusion of memory and
lament, of loved ones and impossible youth, clutching
the stick in the middle he stumbles bowed over the
fields, a life of my own I tried, in vain, never any
but his, worth nothing, because of me, he said it
wasn't one, it was, still is, the same, I'm still inside,
the same, I'll put faces in his head, names, places,
churn them all up together, all he needs to end,

phantoms to flee, last phantoms, to flee and to pursue, he'll confuse his mother with whores, his father with a roadman named Balfe, I'll feed him an old curdog, a mangy old curdog, that he may love again, lose again, ruinstrewn land, little panic steps

I GAVE UP
BEFORE BIRTH

I GAVE up before birth, it is not possible otherwise, but birth there had to be, it was he, I was inside, that's how I see it, it was he who wailed, he who saw the light, I didn't wail, I didn't see the light, it's impossible I should have a voice, impossible I should have thoughts, and I speak and think, I do the impossible, it is not possible otherwise, it was he who had a life, I didn't have a life, a life not worth having, because of me, he'll do himself to death, because of me, I'll tell the tale, the tale of his death, the end of his life and his death, his death alone would not be enough, not enough for me, if he rattles it's he who will rattle, I won't rattle, he who will die, I won't die, perhaps they will bury him, if they find him, I'll be inside, he'll rot, I won't rot, there will be nothing of him left but bones, I'll be inside, nothing left but dust, I'll be inside, it is not possible otherwise, that's how I see it, the end of his life and his death, how he will go about it, go about coming to an end, it's impossible I should know, I'll know, step by step, impossible I should tell, I'll tell, in the present, there will be no more talk of me, only

45

of him, of the end of his life and his death, of his burial if they find him, that will be the end, I won't go on about worms, about bones and dust, no one cares about them, unless I'm bored in his dust, that would surprise me, as stiff as I was in his flesh, here long silence, perhaps he'll drown, he always wanted to drown, he didn't want them to find him, he can't want now any more, but he used to want to drown, he usen't to want them to find him, deep water and a millstone, urge spent like all the others, but why one day to the left, to the left and not elsewhither, here long silence, there will be no more I, he'll never say I any more, he'll never say anything any more, he won't talk to anyone, no one will talk to him, he won't talk to himself, he won't think any more, he'll go on, I'll be inside, he'll come to a place and drop, why there and not elsewhere, drop and sleep, badly because of me, he'll get up and go on, badly because of me, he can't stay still any more, because of me, he can't go on any more, because of me, there's nothing left in his head, I'll feed it all it needs.

CLOSED SPACE

CLOSED place. All needed to be known for say is known. There is nothing but what is said. Beyond what is said there is nothing. What goes on in the arena is not said. Did it need to be known it would be. No interest. Not for imagining. Place consisting of an arena and a ditch. Between the two skirting the latter a track. Closed place. Beyond the ditch there is nothing. This is known because it needs to be said. Arena black vast. Room for millions. Wandering and still. Never seeing never hearing one another. Never touching. No more is known. Depth of ditch. See from the edge all the bodies on its bed. The millions still there. They appear six times smaller than life. Bed divided into lots. Dark and bright. They take up all its width. The lots still bright are square. Appear square. Just room for the average sized body. Stretched out diagonally. Bigger it has to curl up. Thus the width of the ditch is known. It would have been in any case. Sum the bright lots. The dark. Outnumbered the former by far. The place is already old. The ditch is old. In the beginning it was all bright. All bright lots. Almost

49

touching. Faintly edged with shadow. The ditch seems straight. Then reappears a body seen before. A closed curve therefore. Brilliance of the bright lots. It does not encroach on the dark. Adamantine blackness of these. As dense at the edge as at the centre. But vertically it diffuses unimpeded. High above the level of the arena. As high above as the ditch is deep. In the black air towers of pale light. So many bright lots so many towers. So many bodies visible on the bed. The track follows the ditch all the way along. All the way round. It is on a higher level than the arena. A step higher. It is made of dead leaves. A reminder of beldam nature. They are dry. The heat and the dry air. Dead but not rotting. Crumbling into dust rather. Just wide enough for one. On it no two ever meet.

OLD EARTH

OLD earth, no more lies, I've seen you, it was me, with my other's ravening eyes, too late. You'll be on me, it will be you, it will be me, it will be us, it was never us. It won't be long now, perhaps not tomorrow, nor the day after, but too late. Not long now, how I gaze on you, and what refusal, how you refuse me, you so refused. It's a cockchafer year, next year there won't be any, nor the year after, gaze your fill. I come home at nightfall, they take to wing, rise from my little oaktree and whirr away, glutted, into the shadows. I reach up, grasp the bough, pull myself up and go in. Three years in the earth, those the moles don't get, then guzzle guzzle, ten days long, a fortnight, and always the flight at nightfall. To the river perhaps, they head for the river. I turn on the light, then off, ashamed, stand at gaze before the window, the windows, going from one to another, leaning on the furniture. For an instant I see the sky, the different skies, then they turn to faces, agonies, loves, the different loves, happiness too, yes, there was that too, unhappily. Moments of life, of mine too, among others, no

53

denying, all said and done. Happiness, what happiness, but what deaths, what loves, I knew at the time, it was too late then. Ah to love at your last and see them at theirs, the last minute loved ones, and be happy, why ah, uncalled for. No but now, now, simply stay still, standing before a window, one hand on the wall, the other clutching your shirt, and see the sky, a long gaze, but no, gasps and spasms, a childhood sea, other skies, another body.

Paris, August 1974